FAIR STREET
My Road to *Voice of Maasai*

*Before I ever crossed an ocean,
I learned the art of exchange on
Fair Street.*

JESSEY JANSEN

Designed by Jacqueline Mennenoh

Voice of Maasai music label and talent platform is dedicated to producing uplifting East African music and multimedia storytelling through co-writes, collaborations, and original compositions.

Copyright © 2026 by Jessey Jansen

All rights reserved, including the right to reproduce this book or portions thereof in any form whatsoever. For information about permissions to reproduce sections from this book, please contact Jessey Jansen at jessey@littleladystudio.com or 414-272-9999. Voice of Maasai brand is owned by Little Lady Studio LLC, 4713 Ruiz St, Austin TX.

Library of Congress Control Number: 2026901355

Published by Little Lady Studio
Authored by Jessey Jansen
Book design by Jacqueline Mennenoh

ISBN: 979-8-9942834-2-4

www.voiceofmaasai.com

For my late parents, who taught me that creativity is a kind of solution. And for Morgan, Irene, David, Pendo P, ChuChu, Little L; friends in Tanzania whose giving souls were taken far too soon.

Table of Contents

INTRODUCTION	1
PART 1: Origins and Intentions	3
The Note That Found Me First	5
The Road That Asked Me to Listen	15
Untying My Living Knot – Weaving Bridges	19
PART 2: Serengetidipity, The Sound of Collaboration	23
Our First Recording	25
Once the Mics Went Silent, the Mission Deepened	35
The First Album and Beginning Band of Believers	41
PART 3: Release and Reach	47
Meetings of Songs and Minds	49
From Local Echoes to Global Ears	59
From Storybook Wishes to Mzungu Realities	65
PART 4: Resilience, Dream Team, Movement Ignited	73
Resilience in Real Time	75
Dream Team by Design, Not Chance	85
Foundations in Concrete and Community	93
PART 5: Lessons Learned: Field Notes & Practical Takeaways	101
Business Credo: How We Went from Idea to Music Label	102
Closing Notes	109
ACKNOWLEDGMENTS	110
ABOUT THE AUTHOR & FOUNDER	114
ABOUT THE BOOK DESIGNER	115

Fair Street
My Road to *Voice of Maasai*

Before I ever crossed an ocean, I learned the art of exchange on Fair Street in Wautoma, Wisconsin; trading bags of ice for carnival rides, turning our front yard into a parking lot for the county fair, and discovering that with a little hustle and humor, almost anything could be negotiated. My dad taught me that creativity was a kind of currency: use what you have, make it count, and share the win.

Years later, from my home in Texas, that same instinct led me halfway around the world. In the northern highlands of Tanzania, where the savannah meets the sky and songs rise like weather, another kind of exchange began. It started not with a business plan, but with a spark: a conversation between crimson-robed Maasai and a curious woman with more imagination than caution.

What followed became a pursuit, to use music as a bridge across culture, language, and time. This book is a record of that pursuit: how a creative experiment became a living collaboration known as *Voice of Maasai*; and how humor, humility, and persistence built something stronger than profit, a shared resonance.

Inside are first encounters and fragile recordings, power cuts and breakthroughs, and the lessons that taught me what Fair Street once did: equity isn't about even shares, it's about everyone having a place in the song.

A living archive. A collision made possible by creativity. A movement told in music.

> *"We want people to know our story. Can you help?"*

PART 1

Origins and Intentions

CHAPTER 1
The Note That Found Me First ——— 5

CHAPTER 2
The Road That Asked Me to Listen ——— 15

CHAPTER 3
Untying My Living Knot – Weaving Bridges ——— 19

CHAPTER 1

The Note That Found Me First

I grew up on Fair Street, directly across from the county fairgrounds, where the smell of fried sugar mixed with diesel, and every summer the world came roaring in on flatbed trucks. The railroad tracks, *the Line,* cut through our days with a steady pulse, and migrant labor crews moved in and out with the seasons, teaching me early that everyone was trading something—time, skill, or sheer endurance—to make it all work.

My father was an enterprising man, always scheming, always bartering. Once, he traded a boat for an ice cube machine so he could sell ice to the carnies who rolled in each year. My sisters and I would bag it up, haul it across the street, and barter for rides or corn dogs. Pop put us to work, which meant I earned bargaining power, and I loved it. Every exchange was a small adventure, a lesson in how resourcefulness and charm could stretch a dollar further than anyone expected.

But beneath all that hustle lived quieter truths: my father's fragile heart, my mother's lingering illnesses, the unspoken fatigue that shadowed our home. We didn't name it then—we just felt the tension between play and worry, enterprise and exhaustion. Those contradictions taught me how to read a room, adapt quickly, and step in when adults faltered; a living knot woven from delight and difficulty. I wasn't just learning to hustle—I was learning how people hold together.

Twenty years later, that same pulse carried me far from Fair Street to the savannahs below Kilimanjaro, where a different kind of note found me first.

Moshi Tanzania *(August 2, 2011)*

I arrived in Tanzania on a volunteer placement, carrying more than just a suitcase. I came looking for collaboration, for connection built from the ground up. Underneath that search was something that had shaped me all my life, the urge to make things from scratch. Not just projects, but systems, relationships, and frameworks that could hold people together when nothing else did.

Still, I knew what I was: a foreigner, white, easily distrusted here. Cross-cultural work isn't a calling card you hand out, it's a responsibility you earn, slowly, and often awkwardly. I wasn't arriving with answers, only a willingness to listen, learn, and contribute where invited.

My choice of Tanzania had long been seeded in memory, rooted in a childhood fascination with an old Encyclopedia Britannica, one of the few books in our home. On its glossy pages, Africa unfolded: vast savannahs, crimson-clad pastoralists, lives lived to a rhythm I couldn't yet name. That image stayed with me, not as a fantasy, but as a question. Even then, I sensed patterns—visual, cultural, human—that I wanted to understand from within, not from afar.

This journey was an opening into a world that would challenge me, change me, and begin a story I never saw coming.

At 4:00 a.m., roosters announced morning with punctual cuck-a-cuck-a-roos, better timekeepers than any alarm clock. Jet-lagged or not, you didn't argue.

Most of my time was spent at homebase, a quiet compound at the far end of a maze of dusty roads, where small homes stood patched together with tin, wood, and weathered scraps. The air carried the scent of charcoal smoke and the distant laughter of children.

My assignment for the day seemed simple enough: introduce myself to local residents using a well-worn, hand-marked map, and learn a little of their stories in return. But as I stepped toward the gate, curiosity wrestled with a quiet tremor of nerves. The task felt intimate, almost intrusive, I was walking into someone else's story mid-sentence, unsure of the language or the rules.

To steady myself, I leaned into an unusual but strangely effective ritual: ten push-ups before heading out. Not exactly the toolkit of a seasoned cultural ambassador, but the only one I had. Endorphins and awkwardness, a winning combo.

Armed with my Swahili phrasebook, a loosely folded map, and a willingness to fumble through, I stepped out. The midday heat pressed down, dust rose in small clouds with every step, and my first attempts were awkward at best—half mime, half hope. But they were met with grace. Smiles bridged gaps. Laughter came easier than I expected, just like those old carnival days on Fair St when a little nerve and a good joke could get you a free ride.

I wasn't just learning vocabulary. I was learning the architecture of trust, when to speak, when to wait, when a laugh could bridge more than a sentence ever could.

One encounter stayed with me: a radiant fifteen-year-old with a quick laugh and curious eyes. We stumbled through a conversation with simple words, high-fives, and humming melodies when speech failed. Her energy reminded me of my kids' open, unfiltered, and full of rhythm. Our exchange was brief, but it taught me something I hadn't expected, that openness didn't come from my effort to connect, but from her generosity in letting me stumble, laugh, and learn beside her.

The remainder of the day unfolded gently. I practiced bits of conversational Swahili, helped peel vegetables for dinner and learned more about the homebase staff.

By dusk, the air cooled and my thoughts finally slowed. A few fellow volunteers gathered for an outdoor yoga session, and I joined in. The stretching helped release the tension I hadn't realized I was holding. It was a small, steadying act; the kind that reminded me to stay present, to breathe, and to keep listening more than I spoke.

The first days I felt like I was learning to breathe differently, slower, more deliberately. My ears adjusted to new rhythms, cowbells, market chatter, radio static, and the lull of languages not yet familiar. I worked with local organizations, sat in on meetings I barely understood, and kept my mouth shut more than anything, trying to understand the rhythm of a place so unlike where I had come from. The place didn't reveal itself all at once. To be fair, neither did I, I was still figuring out how to order lunch without accidentally proposing marriage.

Behind the Scenes: *Pristine Trails*

Somewhere between craving adventure and needing distraction, a group of volunteers and I ventured into Moshi one weekend. That's where we found Pristine Trails Adventure and Safari; a modest office buzzing with young men whose easy confidence made you believe adventure wasn't just possible, it was waiting.

They sold us trips with a grin, talked in wide hand gestures, and convinced a few of us ladies to book a weekend to Zanzibar. It felt spontaneous, slightly reckless, and exactly the kind of seduction I was open to at the time.

What I didn't know was how essential they would become in my years ahead. They weren't just guides through city streets; they became interpreters of cultural nuance, navigators of unspoken rules, protectors when my curiosity ran too far ahead. They teased me when I tripped over Swahili words, explained everything from rally racing to camel's milk, and reminded me, sometimes gently, sometimes not, that thick skin wasn't optional here. They gave me a glimpse of *Tanzania behind the scenes*, a perspective no guidebook could offer.

The First Note

Days blurred together, light, dust, and discoveries unfolding at their own unhurried pace. As the month waned, a women's collective I'd supported through Cross Cultural Solutions invited me to visit a Maasai community. That simple ask cracked something open. It wasn't the itinerary that stirred me, but the pull of curiosity, the sense that something unseen, unnamed, was waiting just beyond the horizon.

We traveled along winding roads veiled in orange dust, wheels kicking up clouds that dissolved into dry air. Above us, the sun loomed balanced and unrelenting, drawing everything beneath it into a silent, golden orbit. When we arrived, the landscape opened into quiet expectancy. An older man stepped forward, Dr. Ole Kuney, his presence calm and assured. He offered a few words before introducing us to several women of the community.

They stood tall, dignified, adorned in beadwork that caught the light with every movement; shimmering like sunlit rain, grounded with strength. Their welcome was warm, but measured, reminding me that hospitality here carried its own boundaries and protocols.

And then, without cue, without prelude, the air shifted. A procession of about twenty people emerged from the trees, their movements steady, draped in brilliant shúkà cloth of crimson, cobalt, and violet. A low hum rose, guttural and hypnotic, layered voices threading together like something older than language, closer to prayer than to music as I had known it.

There were no instruments. No microphones. Just voice, layered, textured, patient. It wasn't performance; it was presence.

A sound not meant to impress but to center. The tones were deep and utterly untranslatable through the lens I had arrived with.

I stood motionless, absorbing what I could, aware that I didn't fully understand, yet somehow feeling understood. The light softened and space around us felt suspended.

My nose tingled with emotion. I asked one of the mamas if it was traditional Maasai music. She smiled gently.

"*It's who we are,*" she said. "*We don't sing music. We are music.*"

Her words struck deep. Not just curiosity, but a sense of connection. Not the kind that claims ownership or insight, but the kind that recognizes when you've stumbled upon something sacred and whispers: What will you do now that you've heard it?

As the final notes softened into silence, a slender, mature woman stepped forward and gently placed her hand on my shoulder. Her voice was steady, her English careful.

"*We want people to know our story. Can you help?*"

It wasn't a plea. It was a proposal, an invitation offered from a place of dignity, not desperation. They weren't asking me to speak for them; they were challenging me to consider what role I might play in making space for their voices. I was unsure. I didn't know how, but I knew I had to try. I looked into her eyes, feeling the weight of the moment settle between us. My voice came out quieter than I expected, "*let me think.*"

The gathering ended soon after, a fleeting social moment that could have easily faded into memory. But my thoughts kept spinning. Something had shifted. I couldn't stop replaying the music, the words, that moment under the trees.

I felt a thread connect, subtle but strong, between what I had witnessed and what I might help carry forward.

It didn't feel like a goodbye. It felt like an opening.

That night, I couldn't sleep. The sound wasn't just in my ears, it was lodged in my chest like a pulse I hadn't known was missing. It came with a whisper of responsibility; if you're going to carry a voice, you must also learn to carry the silence around it.

As I buckled into my KLM seat, ready to fly home, I knew deep in my bones; this was only the beginning. The very first note.

CHAPTER 2

The Road That Asked Me to Listen

"We don't sing music. We are music."

On the flight home, high above the savannah, the idea took shape; what if we could record their songs, not just to market them, but to honor and extend them? Not to elevate, but to amplify. To build a bridge, not a stage; a living exchange where creativity could sustain community, and enterprise could serve art.

It was improbable, fragile, and a little wild, but it was alive. And sometimes, alive is enough to begin.

In the hum of the KLM cabin, I thought of my late parents; my father's craft and patience, my mother's reverence for story. He had taught us to handle vinyl records like ritual; she had taught us that every voice deserves to be heard. Their lessons stitched themselves into a new promise: to build something durable from sound.

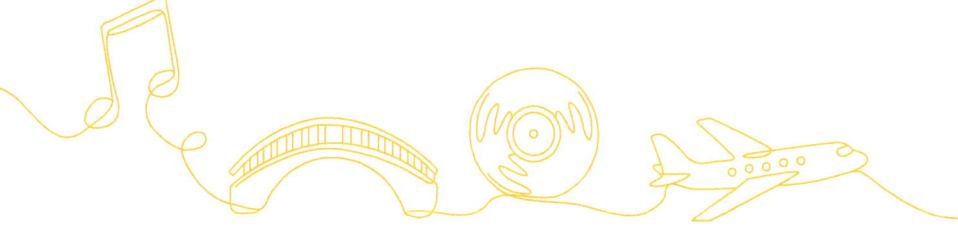

But inspiration alone doesn't move choirs across rural Tanzania. It would take logistics, communication, money, and the entrepreneurial muscle I'd built over years of production work; campaigns for the Green Bay Packers, projects with Team JLo, brand collaborations from beauty to healthcare. Those experiences had taught me how to translate vision into execution, and failure into data.

When I stepped off that long flight—jet-lagged, aching, but newly lit inside—I saw them waiting: my steady husband, bouquet in hand, and my two kids waving in relief and curiosity. Their embrace grounded me after weeks of navigating worlds that stretched me wide. They also reminded me how quickly children grow in six weeks. I'd left with young ones; I returned to miniature philosophers asking, "*So... did you ride a lion?*"

What changed me most wasn't only hearing the music but understanding the context it lived in. These weren't songs designed for applause; they were woven into the rhythm of life. As I listened more closely, I sensed something deeper; the voices carrying continuity were not always the voices shaping decisions.

Patriarchy wasn't theory in Tanzania; it was practice. I admired the women's role in the sound, but admiration alone wasn't enough. Respect required discernment: to understand the social architecture that shaped whose voices traveled and whose stayed local.

The work couldn't be about inserting my vision into their tradition. It had to begin with listening; to the songs, yes, but also to the silence between them. My entrepreneurial instincts wanted to build structure, but structure already existed. My role was not to design; it was to create pathways where dignity could travel with the sound.

Back home, with children's laughter echoing down the hallway and Michael's steady presence beside me, the idea crystallized. What if we could record their songs; capture them in a way that didn't extract but exalted? It felt impossible at first. No roadmap, no music industry background, just a handful of contacts in Tanzania. But the memory of that raw, resonant choir—and the mama who asked, "*Can you help?*"—became my compass.

Slowly, purpose sharpened. This wasn't about producing an album for Western ears. It was about building a living collaboration; mutual, messy, risky, rooted in listening before action. It would demand grit shaped by life, work, and motherhood, balanced with the grace to let others lead.

I didn't know all the steps, but I knew the first one: begin.

One email. One conversation. One kitchen-table brainstorm. That same scrappy instinct I learned back on Fair Street—where creativity was currency and resourcefulness kept everything going—was now steering something bigger.

WhatsApp threads hummed with possibility as messages turned into introductions, bookings, and buses. A liaison carried the idea to the mamas in Remiti, where it was received with curiosity and grace. We confirmed participation, found a choir master, secured a studio in Arusha, arranged lodging, and mapped transport for thirty singers. My husband and I agreed the trip was worth the expense; a risk worth taking.

Everything moved *pole pole*, slowly but surely.

And as the pieces clicked into place, I sensed the truth beneath it all: this work wasn't asking only for my skills, but for the whole story that shaped me.

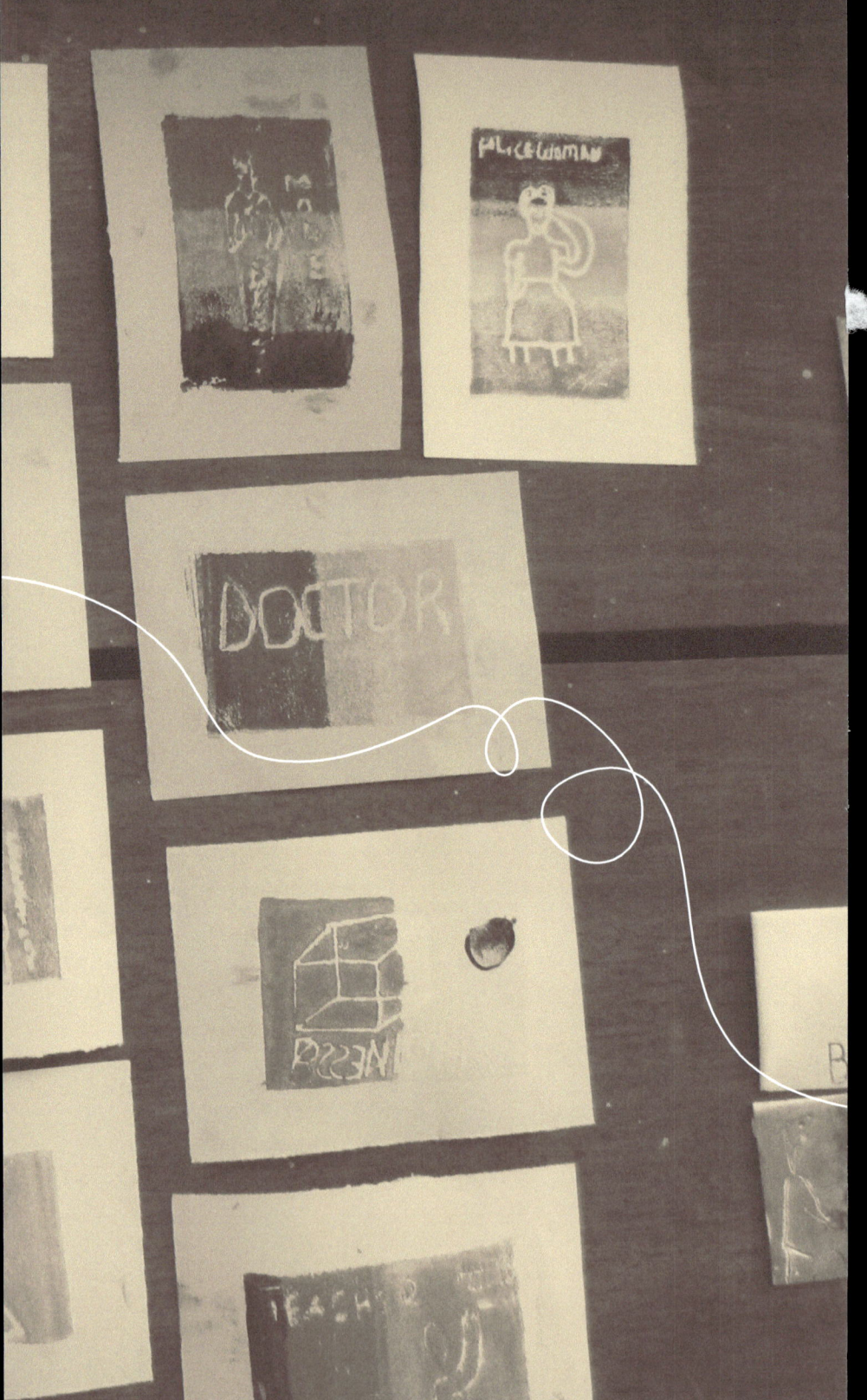

CHAPTER 3

Untying My Living Knot – Weaving Bridges

Some threads tighten with time, woven from pain, hope, and memory. A tangled story of who I was, who I am, and who I'm still becoming. In loosening those threads, I made space to reach outward, to build bridges from my past to my present, from my own heart to others.

Creativity had always been my quiet way through the hard places. It wasn't cultivated in classrooms; it was carved from early responsibility, illness in the household, and the pressure to keep things functioning when life buckled. Fair Street had trained me well: pay attention, improvise solutions, honor your limits, and keep moving even when the ground shifts.

Those instincts would quietly become the compass I carried into adulthood.

By my twenties, life had pulled tight; losing my father, caring for my mother as her health declined, raising children, building a business, ending a marriage. Art arrived not as escape, but as direction. It

helped me untangle the parts of myself that grief and obligation had knotted together. And that steadying force eventually opened a door; a sponsorship, then a volunteer placement in Tanzania.

In 2011, I went not seeking adventure, but understanding. I wanted to see what creativity could build when used in service of community, not commerce. I arrived in Tanzania carrying the instincts shaped by difficult years; listen deeply, tread lightly, build trust slowly.

What happened there shifted something in me. I returned home with more questions than answers, but with a sense that my life had brushed against something meaningful, something unfinished.

So when the question came

"Can you help?"

something in me answered before my mind caught up. Yes.

That yes became the hinge.

In 2012, after months of preparation, I returned to Tanzania with a steadier calm. I carried notebooks and logistics, yes, but also the instincts shaped by years of living knots: listen closely, trade wisely, and treat every interaction as an opportunity to build trust. I didn't yet know that this trip would mark the first notes of a project far bigger than I imagined; a recording session that would become the heartbeat of *Voice of Maasai*.

> "*Creativity is never a solo act—it's a chorus.*"

PART 2

Serengetidipity, The Sound of Collaboration

CHAPTER 4
Our First Recording —————————————————— 25

CHAPTER 5
Once the Mics Went Silent, the Mission Deepened ——— 35

CHAPTER 6
The First Album and Beginning Band of Believers ——— 41

CHAPTER 4

Our First Recording

Some things are not meant to make sense at first.
Ancient voices in a modern studio.
A foreign woman recording songs she can't yet translate.

I called it *Serengetidipity*, when unlikely forces meet in creative communion. A word, a way of living: welcoming the improbable and trusting it to take root. That's how *Voice of Maasai* began.

This isn't about technical production. It's about ceremony, choosing connection over comfort, the road less traveled over the familiar. It is about the moment a fragile idea stepped out of imagination and into sound.

Dream-Makers *(June 30, 2012)*

In life, I've met many kinds of people.
Initiators, who spark movement.
Articulators, who give shape.
Stabilizers, jokers, complainers, balancers, participants.

But every once in a long while, you meet a dream-maker.

Dream-makers are rare. They move quietly, humbly, sprinkling their presence like fine morning dew. They see what others miss. They trust the unseen and invest in the uncertain. They are resourceful, steady in the face of setbacks, and they never shrink from the unknown.

On the flight to Tanzania, nerves frayed, I realized I was not alone. A few of these dream-makers were with me, gifting their wisdom, patience, and belief. That realization steadied me as the jet engines roared and the East African landscape unfurled below: circular bomas like necklaces on the earth, geometric crop fields stretching into symmetry, and the rolling hills of Arusha breaking into view.

I whispered to myself:
"Jessey, get done what you set out to do."

Months of planning might hold. They might not. I stepped off the plane at Kilimanjaro with hope and a simple compass: safety, recognition, belonging. Safety, because collaboration shrivels if people feel exposed. Recognition (yes, vanity too), because everyone wants their contribution seen. Belonging, because without it even strong voices go unheard.

The tarmac shimmered in the late afternoon sun as I descended the stairs, each step carrying both doubt and determination. Inside the small terminal, chaos and rhythm blended, suitcases thudding onto worn belts, voices tumbling in Swahili, the smell of diesel and sweat. Then, through the press of strangers, a familiar face; a young tour guide I'd befriended the summer before, smiling wide, arm raised in welcome.

Relief washed over me as he took my bag and led me to the car. The drive to Arusha was a blur of open road and red earth, children waving from the roadside, the occasional goat darting across the path. Out the window, Mount Meru loomed like a quiet sentinel, watching over every uncertain thought I carried.

I had only two days to shake off jet lag, steady my nerves, and finalize the last fragile pieces of a plan stretched thin across continents. No room for hesitation. No space for doubt. Just the wide Tanzanian sky above me and the steady rhythm of wheels on uneven road reminding me—adventure had already begun.

Day 1: The First Note *(July 02, 2012)*

At 4:30 a.m., twenty-two members of the Remiti Village Choir boarded a cramped dala-dala for the four-hour ride to Arusha. For many, it was their first time leaving home. When the door slid open, the minibus seemed to spill people onto the street; blue wraps, fresh sandals, beaded finery they'd been gifted for the project. Pride shone brighter than the sun.

We met with smiles and steady handshakes. Then I saw her, the mama who'd once asked, *Can you help?* Her smile collapsed the year between us. The answer was still alive—yes.

As we approached the building, a narrow staircase beckoned. With each step, the air thickened; machine oil rising from the mechanic's shop below, punctuated by the clang of metal on metal. The soundscape felt almost ceremonial, and oddly nostalgic—hammers and wrenches marking time like a prelude, a rough rhythm ushering us back to the work we'd begun, an improvised overture of greetings and welcomes.

Memories surged as we climbed, the first time I'd heard their voices. By the time we reached the studio door, the past and present overlapped, humming together like two notes held in harmony. I paused, hand on the frame, sensing that we were not just entering a room, but re-entering a covenant: a promise to turn imagination into sound, and sound into something that could travel farther than any of us alone.

At the top, we entered a dimly lit room where a young recording engineer, Alex Lobulu, sat quietly in the corner, eyes fixed on an aging mixer board like it was sacred.

"*You trust that thing?*" I teased, eyeing the dusty keyboard. Without missing a beat, Alex smirked. "*More than I trust you not to trip over a cable.*" And with that, we were off, humor stitching a quick thread of trust.

Before entering the recording room, each choir member carefully removed their beaded jewelry and blue cloth, the beauty of the culture, temporarily set aside for the sake of clear audio. The beads would have made the microphones sing in ways we didn't want.

They donned their headphones, took their positions. The sound technician gave the cue and I stepped into the control room. And then, it happened.

The first song rose, and the room changed shape. We glanced at one another, near-strangers recognizing the same truth; this would work.

Translation in Triplicate

Before we even began recording, it became clear that our communication would need its own choreography. Most of the choir didn't speak Swahili, let alone English. Instructions moved like a relay race: I spoke in English to Alex, Alex translated into Swahili for the coordinator, and the coordinator translated into Maa for the choir. By the time the words landed, I half expected them to bear no resemblance to what I'd started with.

It turned out to be part comedy, part miracle. I asked Alex to tell the choir to *"stand a little closer to the microphone."* By the time it cycled through, they all stepped back instead. Alex and I just looked at each other and laughed. "*Close enough,*" he said, shrugging. It became our mantra for the week.

Despite the layers of translation, the music didn't get lost. Somehow, it soared past the language barrier. Where words tangled, rhythm carried. Where instructions faltered, laughter stitched the gaps. Double translations weren't a setback, they were part of the adventure, part of the proof that Serengetidipity was alive in the room.

Midday Break: Bread and Resilience

Hours passed: singing, rehearsing, weaving voices into harmony. Then, slowly, the energy shifted; shoulders slumped, rhythms softened, eyes grew distant. Hunger had finally quieted even the music.

Alex spotted a bread vendor outside on a bicycle, grabbed my arm and bolted like we'd discovered buried treasure. Minutes later we came back triumphant, arms full of loaves, grinning as if we'd just pulled off a miracle.

As we passed the loaves around, someone asked a question in Maa. It traveled through the chain—Maa to Swahili, Swahili to English— and landed in my lap as, "*Do you like eating bicycles?*" I blinked, torn between uncertainty and laughter. Alex nearly choked on his tea, waving it off. "*Not bicycles, mandazi. They meant fried bread.*"

From then on, any time something didn't translate cleanly, Alex would grin and whisper, "*Careful, bicycles.*" It became our inside joke, a shorthand for all the ways language failed us but laughter saved us.

We pushed onward. Some songs flowed effortlessly; others needed patient revision. By evening, fatigue returned. I checked the time, 7:30 PM. My taxi back to the hotel would arrive soon, and it wasn't safe to linger after dark.

Then, another hurdle; the original bus scheduled to return the choir refused to come that late. Alex and I traded a look—*of course*. We improvised again, organizing a taxi to shuttle the group in four trips. Our running joke became: *If nothing goes wrong, are we even really recording?*

By 11:30 PM, everyone reached the hostel. Rest was brief; tomorrow, we would rise and sing again.

That night I lay awake, knowing this was not just sound, it was spirit. It was Serengetidipity in bloom: modern equipment and ancient rhythm; city studio and village voice; planning and improvisation; fear and faith.

Day 2: Holding the *Note (July 3, 2012)*

Morning arrived unresolved, like a note held in suspense. The studio manager was late, we turned waiting into laughter, me with a camera, them erupting when "*say cheese*" translated as *"say crazy."* Alex nearly dropped his coffee laughing, *"Careful, they'll think you're the crazy one, mzungu kichaa."*

"Too late," I said. *"That rumor probably started yesterday."*

That, too, is Serengetidipity.

When the manager arrived, we gathered quickly, choir coordinator, Alex, and me. The plan: finish by 3 p.m., transport ready before dusk. The hostel had proven uneasy, nothing dramatic, just subtle tensions, unspoken discomforts, a quiet reminder that we were living between worlds. The choice was clear: finish today.

Back in the booth, the choir sang with renewed fire. In the control room, the choir coordinator leaned toward me, voice low, she was unwell. We called a taxi, retrieved her medication, and paid the hostel bill. While we were gone, the choir pressed on. Tireless. Present. Offering more than voices; offering trust, belief, a piece of themselves no microphone could capture.

By late afternoon, the final notes settled into silence. Exhaustion hung in the air, but so did triumph.

We gathered, speaking slowly across languages, letting patience do the work where words could not. The pauses felt just as important as the phrases, small bridges built out of silence and trust. In the end, what rose between us was not perfect understanding, but a shared commitment: to carry this work forward.

As the last of the choir members shuffled onto the bus, the air hung heavy with dust and the low murmur of voices. Mama stepped toward me, her eyes steady, her hand warm as it found my arm. She leaned close and whispered, *"tenebo oiye," we are together*.

Heat rose behind my eyes.

"Ashe," I managed. Thank you. Small word, full weight.

Beyond the Recording

"Creativity is never a solo act—it's a chorus."

We hadn't just tracked an album; we'd set a cultural motion.
I was the outsider. The divide was real, braided into history.
And yet, they stayed, they sang, they trusted something
neither of us could fully name but both knew mattered.

The choir returned as ambassadors, proof that
tradition and innovation can share breath.

When the studio finally dimmed, I sat in the hush, full of gratitude.
What began as a fragile question had become a testament
to resilience and that improbable gift—Serengetidipity.

Not just sound. Spirit.
Not just memory. Movement.
The first portfolio of songs, honoring tradition, transcending borders.

CHAPTER 5

Once the Mics Went Silent, the Mission Deepened

There's a moment, after the final note fades and the equipment powers down, when silence doesn't feel like absence, it feels like thunder held in the chest. It isn't emptiness; it's reverence. The kind of quiet that makes you aware you've crossed into new territory, like stepping onto a ridge after a hard climb and seeing the horizon crack wide open.

That's what it felt like when we wrapped recording with the Remiti Choir. The microphones powered down, the studio dimmed, but inside me the air still vibrated with their voices, low, soaring, unstoppable. It wasn't just music anymore; it was ignition. Something had shifted, an alchemy of risk and rhythm, of trust and courage. Their voices had taken root in me, not as echoes but as momentum, carrying me forward like the first gust of wind before a storm.

From Curiosity to Collaboration

This project began as curiosity, maybe even naivety, a hunch, a yearning. (Thick skin helps when your big idea sounds ridiculous out loud.) But what unfolded became proof of what can happen when tradition is met with humility and collaboration is treated as listening. Not surface listening, but deep, patient listening that allows trust to grow.

We hadn't just recorded songs. In that shared space, I realized; the work was never only about capturing sound, it was about carrying dignity. About building a system, however fragile, where creativity could be honored and collaboration could thrive.

The Difference Between *About* and *With*

So often, "cultural innovation" is spoken of in glossy terms: fusion, trends, virality. But the real work—the sustainable, ethical work—does not begin with ideas. It begins with relationships. With presence. With showing up again and again. Not only to create, but to witness. To understand. To earn trust.

The Maasai choir reinforced a belief I hold sacred: the most powerful art is never made about people, it is made with them. That difference is everything. It is the line between appropriation and collaboration, between telling someone's story and sharing it together.

I was learning to measure a delicate balance: our universal desire for autonomy, and our equally human need to belong. In this choir, I began to see models of cooperation over competition. Their welcome carried lessons I hadn't anticipated; they became not only collaborators, but teachers, showing me what it means to live in rhythm with one another.

The Rhythm of Imperfection

And let's be honest, ethical collaboration is never seamless. It is not performance; it is process. It means checking your ego at the door, improvising when plans collapse, and learning resilience in small, ordinary ways.

Like a bus that never arrives. A bread vendor who saves the day. A hostel that doesn't feel safe.

Not failures, just part of the rhythm. Each challenge reminded me: flexibility is fidelity. To stay is to respect. (Besides, if nothing went wrong, Alex and I would have had nothing to laugh about.)

I thought often about power, who holds it, who frames the story, who decides what counts as "professional." What if tradition itself is the technology? What if preservation of cultural identity is the most radical form of innovation?

Evidence of a Larger Calling

I began to see this work not as a project, but as cultural reclamation. A small act of resistance against erasure. A contribution to systems that might allow voices to endure long after I step aside. It also required structure: models of fairness, creative enterprise, and reinvestment that could sustain the art itself.

I never wanted to be the voice for anyone. I only wanted to help amplify the voices already there. Which meant the work could not end with one album. It asked for sustained commitment, to accountability, transparency, care. It asked us to measure success not by downloads or applause, but by how many young people in Remiti Village might begin to believe their voices matter.

When the choir returned home, they carried more than recordings. They carried evidence—that bridges can be built without burning origins. That dignity is the most powerful instrument. That legacy is not what we leave behind, but what we lift up while we are still here.

And I returned home changed, too, carrying Serengetidipity in my bones.

Because what we made together was more than music. It was proof.

Proof that creativity, when rooted in respect, can be an act of justice. Proof that collaboration, when shaped by listening, can be a sacred exchange.

This was only the second note.

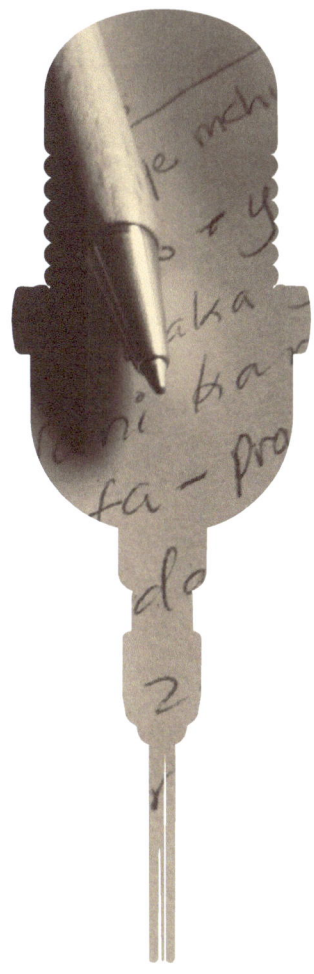

CHAPTER 6

The First Album and Beginning Band of Believers

With the recordings in hand, what lay ahead was not just post-production, it was responsibility. The voices of Remiti had been entrusted to me, and now it was my task to turn raw, living sound into something the world could hear without losing the spirit that made it sacred.

This would not be the work of one person.
It would take a band of believers.

A Patchwork of Believers

We weren't a polished team yet. We were a patchwork of friends, family, fellow artists, and unexpected allies, bound not by contracts or titles, but by conviction. Egos had to be checked at the door, hidden agendas left outside. What we needed instead was selfless camaraderie, the kind that puts mission before recognition.

Conversations unfolded over kitchen tables cluttered with notebooks, and half-drunk mugs of tea. Ideas were scribbled in the margins of plane tickets, on the backs of receipts, and

onto napkins in coffee shops thick with the smell of roast and rain. Some nights, I'd hang up from calls with my voice hoarse from fatigue, but my pulse still racing with possibility.

We weren't fueled by structure; we were fueled by stubborn resolve. A band of believers daring to imagine that music recorded in a modest Tanzanian studio could one day echo across oceans, carrying not just melody, but memory. (And yes, plenty of green tea, not nearly enough sleep.)

Fueling the Vision

Money was an ever-present reality—unglamorous, necessary, and scarce. But scarcity had never stopped me before. I had built small businesses from scratch, pitched to CEOs, and managed campaigns with little more than vision and grit. That same fire carried me here.

I turned every corner into opportunity. I hosted intimate community gatherings where stories carried as much weight as sales. I sold handmade jewelry, each piece strung with the hope of financing another session. I leaned on the generosity of friends who believed in the audacity of the dream. And when a new fan showed curiosity, I didn't just hand them an album, I designed a Tanzanian travel experience that carried them straight into the heart of our story.

Each dollar raised was more than currency; it was proof. Proof that people could, and would, believe in something built on sincerity, creativity, and respect. Every contribution became a small adventure of its own, a reminder that entrepreneurship isn't only about numbers, it's about resilience, imagination, and daring to keep moving when the map runs out.

Listening Before Sharing

When the first mixes were finally due, I caught myself refreshing my inbox too often, half-hoping, half-dreading what would arrive. Alex worked quietly, no updates, no small talk, just long stretches of silence that tested my trust more than I wanted to admit.

I reminded myself that follow-through doesn't always come with fanfare. On Fair Street, I'd learned that good work often happens behind closed doors, in garages, kitchens, and small rooms that smell like effort.

When his files finally landed, I exhaled. The sound was raw but honest, alive in a way that polish can't fake. I gathered a few trusted colleagues and designers, asking them to listen with sharp ears and open hearts. What worked? What didn't? What felt true?

As the songs looped, I filled notebooks with observations, circling back to the same lesson over and over: perfection wasn't the goal. What mattered was honoring the choir's voices, and trusting that Alex, in his own quiet way, had done the same.

A Promise Carried Back

By 2013, Tanzania was inked onto my calendar once more. But this time I wasn't returning with only sketches and hope. I was returning with something tangible: the completed "soft-launch" album.

The very songs entrusted to me in that small Arusha studio were now pressed into permanence—ready to travel farther, to be heard, and to give back. What began as an exchange of voices was becoming a cycle of value, where music itself could carry the promise forward.

And this time, I wouldn't be alone. A fellow traveler had signed on, drawn by a journey that blended adventure with purpose: a Serengeti safari, a Kilimanjaro trek, and at its heart, a choir's voice rising into the world.

44 - The First Album and Beginning Band of Believers

> *What started as an album was evolving into a social enterprise, a living collaboration grounded in shared values.*

PART 3

Release and Reach

CHAPTER 7
Meetings of Songs and Minds —————— 49

CHAPTER 8
From Local Echoes to Global Ears —————— 59

CHAPTER 9
From Storybook Wishes to Mzungu Realities —————— 65

CHAPTER 7

Meetings of Songs and Minds

There is a quiet vulnerability in bringing something back to where it began.

In June 2013, I returned to Tanzania, not empty-handed, but carrying the first finished album; proof that a fragile idea born in a modest studio could survive distance, doubt, and translation.

Alongside me was a new supporter making her first journey to Africa. She wasn't just a traveler; she was a witness. Together, we would climb Mount Kilimanjaro, hand-deliver the album to the choir, and close with a Serengeti safari. Part celebration, part pilgrimage.

Arrival came with a tradition of my own—my friend and guide, Mussa, scooping me up from the airport and taking me straight to dance in Moshi. Jet lag dissolved in rhythm. The night air smelled of dust, the streets alive with laughter and the soft hum of voices blending into song. It was immersion, an immediate surrender to Tanzania's pulse.

Travel here always demanded more than itineraries. Secure pockets for safety. Good boots for uneven paths. Wipes and

a jacket for Kilimanjaro's cool nights. Power outages were more nuisance than obstacle, something I'd learned to adapt to, just as I once did growing up in Wisconsin when bills went unpaid. Even journaling shifted; notes typed quickly into emails or drafts, hedges against the blackout's sudden hush.

In time, I realized what held me most wasn't logic, but rhythm. Not only the rhythm of music, but of life itself, the rise and fall of days stitched together by confidence, curiosity, patience, and grace. Here, I wasn't simply a visitor. I was learning, absorbing, and being reshaped by a tempo older and wiser than my own.

Kilimanjaro: Recognition in a Tent *(2013)*

I thought the best way to ease my guest into culture shock was to start with something physical. She landed on Thursday, and by Friday we were on Kilimanjaro. (In retrospect, aggressive. In the moment, pure adrenaline.)

The drive to the trailhead was punishing, each jolt over rocks and ruts churning my late-night party exhaustion into nausea. I clenched my jaw and held on until the vehicle stopped, but the moment my boots hit the ground I doubled over, dry-heaving into the dust. *Great lead Jessey*, I scolded myself. If my guest wasn't already nervous about the journey ahead, this probably didn't help. I straightened, forced a grin, and pressed forward. Leadership, I reminded myself, isn't about feeling strong, it's about showing up anyway.

At the base of the mountain, a chorus of song greeted us, rising against the silhouette of Kilimanjaro. A team of Pristine guides and porters stood ready, steady hands and wide smiles promising they would carry us as much as our own endurance would. Their voices wrapped around us like a blessing as we set off on the seven-day Lemosho route, excitement and apprehension braided together with every step.

Nights on the mountain carried their own weight:

thin air, bone-deep cold, and wind scraping canvas. Our dinner tent glowed faintly, lantern light flickering across tired faces. That's when it happened. One overconfident bite of popcorn and, crack. My crown popped right off. On Kilimanjaro. I froze, pretending nothing happened, then slipped the tooth into my pocket like contraband. Alex would've laughed himself hoarse if he'd been there. Instead, I laughed quietly to myself: climbing Africa's tallest peak with spare teeth stashed in my jacket. Thick skin, apparently, wasn't just metaphorical.

Moments later, the tent fell into a different kind of hush. That evening, the guides and porters joined us for dinner, an uncommon crossing of the invisible lines that usually separated travelers from workers.

One porter, eyes lowered but voice steady, whispered, "*This is the best day of my life.*" His words carried the quiet pride of being invited in for the first time; sharing a meal not as labor, but as equals. Across the camp table, Mussa caught my eye, a knowing glance that needed no translation. In that instant, I felt it again; that rare alignment of chance and meaning, *Serengetidipity*.

The tent seemed to inhale and hold its breath, conversation

stilled. It wasn't performance, it was raw truth, carried on the back of endless climbs, heavy loads, and silent resilience. In that hush, stories surfaced, one by one, not rehearsed accounts, but fragments of loss, of longing, of what still burned inside each of us.

When my turn came, I spoke softly of why I was there: to return an album of Maasai voices, recorded in a modest studio above a mechanic's shop, so their songs could travel farther than any of us. Words felt fragile in the mountain air, yet something shifted as they settled.

By morning, the porters' songs rang louder, brighter, echoing across ridges as if dignity itself had been unshackled. Beneath Kilimanjaro's shadow, its glacier catching dawn, I understood: this project was never only about sound. It was about recognition. About belonging. About bridges strong enough that no one had to cross alone.

Remiti Village: A Return in Song

The red earth road wound its way into Remiti, each bump and bend tightening the knot in my chest. My heart pounded, not from the ride, but from the question echoing in my mind: after all this time, *would they still trust me?* Would the months of silence feel like absence, or betrayal?

Then I saw him, Dr. Ole, standing tall, steady, and smiling, a compass pointing true north. He clasped my hand, and with that, ushered us back into the community that had once placed faith in a stranger's improbable idea.

The choir did not greet us with hesitation, but with sound, voices rising in a wave that seemed to split the air itself. Their welcome was resolute, radiant. Elders sat wrapped in quiet dignity, their walking sticks planted firmly in the dust. Women stood draped in shúkà cloth of crimson and cobalt, beadwork catching the light like constellations. Children lingered wide-eyed at the edges, laughter just beneath the surface.

And then, through the chorus, I saw her—the mama whose question had started it all. She moved toward me, smiling, her eyes steady. As we embraced, she whispered again: "*tenebo oiye, we are together.*"

The rhythm of Maasai life surrounded us: smoke curling from cooking fires, the low murmur of cattle beyond the huts, dust rising with every shuffle of feet. Gifts were exchanged, food, jewelry, cloth, each offering not transaction, but testament.

A formal meeting was convened, not as hollow ritual but as an act of dignity, a declaration that every voice mattered.

With Dr. Ole translating, I spoke. My words trembled, but my intent was steady—I had returned to continue what we began, to carry their voices farther. Then, with hands shaking ever so slightly, I pressed play.

From the small speakers, their songs rose, recorded above a mechanic's shop, carried across oceans, now circling back home. Faces lit. Pride flickered. Trust, tested by time, began to glow again.

Before leaving, we didn't exchange contracts or paperwork, only words. A long, careful conversation underlined by trust. The agreement was simple; we'd carry the work forward together, giving the music visibility, awareness, and, if we were lucky, the chance for sales that could circle back home. But I also knew how fragile that kind of promise could be. When people see a finished product, they see possibility, and sometimes, personal opportunity. Still, I chose to believe in the strength of our understanding, that what we had sealed in song was stronger than ink.

That day reminded me—trust is not earned by promises alone. It is earned by returning. By listening. By proving that distance cannot dissolve the bond of *tenebo oiye*.

Serengeti: Wonder and Warning

Our final stop was the Serengeti. Elephants lumbered across golden plains, lions stretched in the heat, the horizon pulsed with rhythm as old as time. For a moment, it felt like the journey had closed in perfect symmetry.

Then came the message. A quiet warning passed through a contact—the work we'd entrusted forward had slipped off course. Someone loosely tied to the project was trying to claim it as her own. My stomach sank, not just from frustration, but from recognition.

I'd learned early that when value enters the picture, so does temptation. This wasn't theft in the literal sense, it was the tug-of-war between collaboration and control, between shared purpose and personal gain. A quiet reckoning: good faith can shift without warning. Creativity may be born of inspiration, but it stays alive through the art of negotiation.

The Serengeti gave me both wonder and warning. I had come chasing possibility, but it was clarity I left with. Passion could spark a vision, but it wouldn't sustain it. We would need more than goodwill, it needed structure, strategy, and discernment.

The same instincts that once helped me navigate clients, contracts, and production timelines now applied here: who to trust, when to pause, and how to protect something fragile without smothering its growth. The landscape stretched endless before me, reminding me that dreams don't just need heart, they need a backbone.

What Carried Forward

At this point, I could have shipped the CDs to the choir and called it a job well done. But the promise I'd made, to the woman who had asked *Can you help us share our story?* kept tugging at me. So did the deeper pull to keep shaping what we'd started:

a framework for collaboration built on real human connection. The magnitude of it didn't scare me, it steadied me.

From then on, I promised myself greater care with those who joined, learning to see who truly aligned and who only sought to take. Each exchange became both lesson and test: when to lean in, when to step back, when silence spoke louder than any word.

Trust wasn't built in contracts. It brewed slowly, like chai on verandas, sealed in shared laughter during long, dusty drives, reinforced through small, consistent acts of respect. Negotiating nuance meant more than language; it meant noticing hierarchies, honoring elders, and creating space for women's voices even when systems tried to quiet them.

Back home, the kids didn't ask about jet lag. They wanted to know, "*Did they like it?*" Michael, ever the realist, reminded me to tell it straight, the missteps, the tensions, the joy, because authenticity is the only bridge sturdy enough to cross oceans.

By then, what had begun as a simple idea had taken on a name— *Voice of Maasai*. I created the brand to carry more than music: it would stand for respect, transparency, and accountability. What started as an album was evolving into a social enterprise, a living collaboration grounded in shared values. Not only songs, but sound carrying purpose. Not only recordings, but bridges strong enough to bear weight across cultures and time.

And yes, when I finally sat in that dentist's chair, my rogue crown was glued neatly back in place. Proof that what we carry forward isn't only philosophy or memory, but the small, funny reminders that we were really there, doing the work, learning as we went, holding it all together with a little Fair Street ingenuity.

CHAPTER 8

From Local Echoes to Global Ears

The first album didn't just land on CDs, it landed in conversations, inboxes, and playlists far beyond the foothills of Kilimanjaro. Every new listener felt like proof that the idea had legs. I could feel the brand forming, an energy with momentum. But with each share came a sharper question: *how do I scale without losing what's soulful?*

The answer required more than vision. It meant understanding the mechanics: catalog strategy, licensing, metadata, and all the unglamorous scaffolding that allows art to travel with integrity. It meant standing steady in the crosswinds of collaboration and commerce, balancing cultural sensitivity with entrepreneurial rigor.

Being the Minority, Seeing the Divide

Moving through Tanzania as a visitor, and often the only *mzungu* (foreigner) in the room, trained my senses fast. Eyes lingered; assumptions surfaced. "Minority" wasn't just racial; it was economic, situational, and sometimes moral. Patriarchal structures decided who spoke first and last. Religion framed daily life in ways I couldn't replicate. Around it all—the mzungu divide, where too many foreigners came to rescue and ended up extracting instead.

My rule became simple: *notice patterns, name power, refuse the hero costume.* Build *with*, not *about*.

Meanwhile, the friction of daily life: transport stalls, power cuts, broken plumbing, slow permits, wasn't an inconvenience; it was the reality. Navigating it required confidence, courtesy, and a patience that felt like endurance training.

Kickstarter & Distribution *(2014)*

That first "soft-launch" album revealed what every creative venture eventually does: sparks need structure, and structure needs support.

Back in Austin, I turned the kitchen table into a think tank. With a reliable Wi-Fi connection and a mug of ambition, I built a Kickstarter to raise funds and test traction. Each pledge was both data and belief.

Kyle stuffed envelopes. Niosha called out bad design choices ("too busy, try again"). Michael, as always, stripped my pitch down to its clear, beating heart.

Together we built a *band of believers*, stretching from Austin to Arusha, from coffee shops to corporate desks.

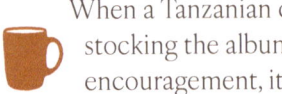

When a Tanzanian distributor expressed interest in stocking the album in gift shops and lodges, it wasn't just encouragement, it was validation. I started sketching a scalable framework: distribution channels, licensing, catalog management, a workflow that protected both artistry and dignity. The goal wasn't simply to sell songs, but to create a pathway where cultural value could move freely and without distortion.

Intention and Improvisation
(Moshi–Arusha, May/June 2014)

Rainstorms cut the Wi-Fi. Power blinked off mid-email. I slept anyway, tomorrow needed a clear head.

Dr. Ole greeted me at Union Café with his usual calm and daughters in tow, sharp, ambitious, ready to change the world. Mussa, my constant translator of Tanzanian reality, guided me through roads, rituals, and rally races, still laughing at my Swahili slipups. He was more than a driver; he was a barometer for what mattered.

By day, I built structure, meetings, strategy, productivity plans. By night, I learned the art of improvisation: conversations at Le Patio under mango trees, introductions over chai, cross-cultural brainstorms that started as small talk and ended as ideas worth chasing.

The week unspooled in rhythm, plans breaking and reforming like jazz. A meeting that fell through led to a new collaborator. A wrong turn revealed a recording studio tucked behind an Ethiopian café. When a lodge manager invited me to a red-carpet event, I showed up in mud-spattered jeans and a grin. Two worlds colliding, and somehow it worked.

That's the thing about practical creativity: you plan, but you also listen, to the moment, to the people, to the current of chance that's often smarter than strategy.

Expanding the Circle

Recording the first songs was one thing; ensuring no one was forgotten after the applause was another. Word spread. Maasai singers, poets, and storytellers reached out, sometimes through mutual friends, sometimes through a brave message sent on borrowed Wi-Fi. Travelers carried the CDs home and wrote back with wonder. Small cultural orgs noticed, not for novelty, but for authenticity. The circle widened, believer by believer.

Storytelling as Advocacy

Between trips, I built an online home that reflected our values, rooted, human, and refreshingly unslick. I uploaded session photos, shared essays on collaboration, posted stories about bread vendors on bicycles and nights when the power died but the singing didn't. It wasn't marketing, it was transparency as advocacy. *Here are the voices. Here's why they matter.*

Sometimes I typed those posts while stirring pasta or hiding in the laundry room for five quiet minutes. The work wove through ordinary life, the way real purpose often does.

Guarding the Fabric

We were still at the edge of possibility. The platform was a foundation, not a finish line. As the music traveled farther, so did the risks, ego, exploitation, misunderstanding. Scale without care could unravel the very thread that made the work worth doing.

So, I tuned the system like a song: reward integrity, sidestep ego, protect women's participation, listen for who holds power even when they aren't speaking. Safety, belonging, and vanity are human levers, design around them. Let dignity stay the north star, not speed.

The next chapter wouldn't be about proving we could be heard. It would be about protecting *how* we listened, about building resonance that could travel farther without losing its roots.

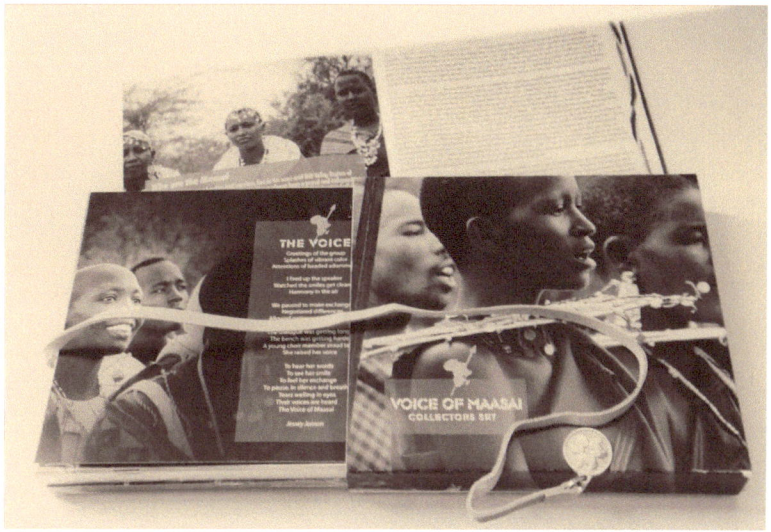

CHAPTER 9

From Storybook Wishes to Mzungu Realities

The next stage wasn't about chasing opportunity; it was about protecting what we'd built so it could breathe and expand. Every partnership was a delicate weave of trust and creativity. Pull too hard in one direction, and the fabric could fray. Growth had to stretch without losing its thread.

Operating in Tanzania always demanded awareness. Police checkpoints were routine. Bribes were not theoretical. Safety was never assumed. It was a dance, one foot grounded in my own sense of home, the other learning East Africa's unpredictable rhythm.

And still, I carried a private daydream: that one day a world-famous artist would call out of the blue, eager to collaborate. That Maasai voices might suddenly climb global charts.

Reality, of course, wrote in subtler ink.

Constellations of Our Own (2015)

Even without celebrity spotlights, we'd built our own constellation of stars. *Voice of Maasai* was becoming recognizable, drawing dreamers, skeptics, and quiet believers into its orbit. Fans wrote to say the music gave them courage to start something of their own. Industry peers leaned closer, curious about these harmonies from the savannah.

At home, I hustled harder than ever: walking trade-show floors, pitching between panels, swapping stories with anyone who'd listen. I wasn't just learning; I was translating passion into language that industry ears could understand. Each conversation was a small act of advocacy, proof that creativity and commerce didn't have to be enemies.

My family became part of that constellation. Kyle and Niosha set up merch tables, managed backer lists, and offered unfiltered critiques (*"too wordy, Mom"*). Michael was my sounding board and sanity check; steady, skeptical in all the right ways, and the one who could turn my hundred tangled thoughts into one clear path forward. Together, we weren't holding the line; we were widening the circle.

Nemaa & the GM Meeting *(2016)*

In 2016, Michael joined me in Tanzania for the first time, a collision of worlds. In Moshi, I introduced him to Dominick, my distributor, who was deep in preparations for a Valentine's gala that looked more royal ball than business meeting. Sequined gowns, linen-draped tables, and the hum of Swahili love songs. We were ushered in as VIPs. Michael caught my eye from across the table, half amused, half stunned: *What have you gotten me into?*

I grinned. *"Welcome to my double life."*

From Moshi's surreal celebrations, we set off with Pristine Trails for the Serengeti, where the land opened in full theater, acacias like ink strokes across the horizon, wildebeest shifting like tides, giraffes moving in quiet procession.

At the Four Seasons lodge, we were invited to a Maasai vocal performance. The lead singer, Nemaa Koshuma, stepped forward, his voice rising in a falsetto so pure it seemed to slice the air itself. For a moment, even the wind held its breath. I leaned toward Michael and whispered, *"We have to record his voice."*

The next morning, instinct kicked in. I wasn't just a listener; I was a builder. I tracked down the general manager, laid out the vision, and asked if he'd help coordinate studio time. No slides, no speeches, just Fair Street pragmatism in action: *act while the spark's still hot.*

A week later, we were in Arusha introducing Nemaa to Alex. The shift from savannah to studio felt dizzying, but the sound bridged both worlds. His voice floated above the rhythm like dawn wind, carrying Maasai roots with a hint of island lilt. Alex worked the board with his usual quiet focus, sculpting the mix until it felt alive. When the GM heard the first tracks, he ordered custom CDs for the lodge gift shop, proof that listening well can lead to opportunity.

Michael just shook his head, half laughing, half proud.
"Only you could turn a safari into a studio session."

First Official Music Video *(2017)*

Momentum demanded more than sound, it needed image. In 2017, I returned to film our first official music video, *Embattled Land*, Nemaa's ode to tradition and modern life as a Serengeti mechanic.

For Alex, it was his first flight. He pressed to the window as the earth dropped away, eyes wide with wonder. By the time we landed, fear had turned to exhilaration.

We carried cameras and conviction into the open plains. Dust swirled, dancers stamped the earth, Nemaa's voice rose to meet the horizon. Behind the lens, Alex kept up a stream of quiet jokes that cracked the tension and made the singers smile bigger than choreography alone ever could. Sweat stung, the light was perfect, and I knew—this wasn't preservation anymore, it was amplification. And laughter, as usual, was the glue.

The Mzungu Reality

In Tanzania, I could never escape what I was, the *mzungu*, the white outsider in the room. My presence shifted chemistry, sometimes subtly, sometimes not. I learned to read cues: a glance, a pause, a politeness laced with doubt. Some days it grounded me in humility; others it left me raw.

With time, I found my footing, not to dominate or disappear, but to create conditions where the work could stand without me. To hold space without becoming the story. It was a balance of confidence and restraint, a discipline, not a stance.

And sometimes it meant laughing at myself; at my tangled Swahili, my cultural misfires, the way locals could turn my confusion into a chorus of laughter. Thick skin wasn't optional. It was just part of the uniform.

Sharpen the Collective *(2018)*

A year later, over tea in Arusha, two young men approached to praise our work. By the time our cups were empty, we'd mapped a new recording session, this time with female artists from Dar es Salaam.

It wasn't just about adding new voices. It was about widening perspective. Every fresh collaborator sharpened the whole. Each session tested adaptability as much as artistry, proof that growth doesn't come from repeating success, but from daring the next verse.

From Wish to Work

Our storybook wish was never about luck. It was about building something meaningful enough that others chose to join. Each connection and melody became a small test of balance, how to grow without unraveling, how to keep the fabric taut but flexible.

By then, I understood: protecting the heart of the work meant placing it in more hands, not fewer, hands that shaped with care, even when they challenged mine. The dream was no longer mine alone. It was a shared chorus, built by design, not by chance.

> *It's like working with a living knot; tightening under pressure, loosening with patience, reshaping each time you touch it.*

PART 4

Resilience, Dream Team, Movement Ignited

CHAPTER 10
Resilience in Real Time — 75

CHAPTER 11
Dream Team by Design, Not Chance — 85

CHAPTER 12
Foundations in Concrete and Community — 93

CHAPTER 10

Resilience in Real Time

Over time, resilience has taken on a different shape in me. In the beginning, it meant endurance; the steady, sometimes stubborn act of holding on. But years of creative work, cultural exchange, and personal loss have reshaped that meaning.

Resilience now feels quieter, more measured. It's the ability to draw from experience and recognize what no longer requires reaction. To say, with calm certainty, "*That's not necessary.*" The earned understanding that energy, like trust, must be protected to be sustained. What once was powered by grit is now guided by grace.

Injury and Sickness

In 2019, a torn Achilles grounded my rhythm of journeys to Tanzania. Months later, the world itself came to a halt. Borders closed, flights vanished, and the hum of studios and dusty roads was replaced with silence as COVID-19 remade the map.

Then another rupture: the storming of the U.S. Capitol exposed fractures at home. In Tanzania, President Magufuli's denial of the virus created an eerie hush, even as illness quietly spread through villages. Fear and misinformation traveled faster than truth. Meanwhile, climate disasters raged, justice movements rose, and every plan bent beneath uncertainty.

Yet amid all that chaos, we returned to what had always steadied us: creativity as connective tissue. Honest, collaborative, human. When the world felt bent toward outrage, we met it with rhythm. When silence pressed in, we answered with sound.

For us, resilience wasn't survival; it was adaptation. The art of finding tempo when the music changes.

Knots of Goodwill

Resilience rarely looks clean. Those new setbacks offered time to pause, to reflect on the work, to check in with myself, and to clarify what I was truly willing to offer: safety, skills, money, emotional support, guidance, connections.

Part of the reality of work built on goodwill and trust is that patterns of financial dependency can emerge. Repeated requests will happen. The "*world pause*" gave me space to reset boundaries, to become more resource-wise, to measure generosity against sustainability.

It's like working with a living knot; tightening under pressure, loosening with patience, reshaping each time you touch it. Some days it feels impossible to undo. But slowly, persistence reveals new strength in the fibers.

That became our rhythm: not breaking through but weaving forward.

By 2019, collaboration had already stretched beyond our music. When the lockdowns arrived, we pivoted, hosting online community art competitions, local radio tours, online accreditation programs, and quiet reflection on what mattered most. Imagination became both resource and refuge, stretching our capacity to offer something new, inclusive, and rooted in the public good.

New Murals, New Networks

In 2020, Wachata Crew arrived from Dar es Salaam to paint a towering mural on Krokon Road—a radiant woman, both life-giver and guide. She embodied what I call the *C-Factor*; creativity shaping confidence, confidence building character, character strengthening community.

Coordinating the effort was Rukia Kurwa, a young creative force I had first met years earlier at the Mount Meru Hotel. Even then, her sharp eye and restless energy hinted at something bigger, a drive to connect art with purpose.

Working side by side with the muralists, she kept the process flowing: securing space, smoothing logistics, and making sure the project spoke not just to passersby, but to the community whose stories it represented.

As the spray paint hissed and colors leapt onto the concrete, Rukia's presence grounded the chaos. She translated between visions and realities, ensuring that the radiant figure rising on Krokon Road wasn't just another piece of public art, but a symbol rooted in local pride.

Watching her lead with such poise and clarity, I felt the generational thread tighten, proof that the *Voice of Maasai* was no longer only mine to carry forward. Leaders like Rukia were already shaping its next verse.

That same year, *Beyond Music*, a global platform uniting artists across borders, invited us in. Their mission to create from connection, not formula, felt like discovering another branch of our own tree.

New Voices, New Currents

Through *Beyond Music*—a global platform uniting artists across borders—I began searching for collaborators whose artistry carried both cultural depth and creative range. I spent weeks studying the network: reading artist profiles, watching performance clips, listening late into the night for that rare balance between rooted tradition and fearless experimentation.

That's how I found Msafiri Zawose, one of Tanzania's leading Gogo musicians and the son of the legendary Dr. Hukwe Zawose, whose work had long been a national treasure and an international bridge for Tanzanian music. Msafiri's mastery of the ilimba (traditional thumb piano) and his ability to fuse ancestral rhythms with modern soundscapes immediately struck me. He wasn't chasing trends; he was expanding tradition.

I reached out, explaining the mission of *Voice of Maasai* and why I believed his artistry could strengthen the label's growing portfolio. He understood instinctively, the shared purpose of cultural preservation through innovation.

Over four COVID-masked, music-filled days in Arusha, Msafiri and Alex blended Gogo tradition with rap verses, layered harmonies, and fearless improvisation. The sessions were electric; equal parts heritage and experiment. The tracks carried urgency: rooted in the red earth of Dodoma yet alive to the pulse of a changing world.

That same year brought floods that nearly swallowed the studio. Still, we unveiled the mural in Arusha, released new tracks, launched radio tours, and upgraded equipment to capture stories with sharper clarity.

Our journey expanded not in flashes of fame, but through deliberate steps of connection and care.

A Decade Marked

By 2021, the rhythm of multiple trips each year had given way to unplanned silence. For two years, borders stayed closed, plans dissolved, and what had once been momentum became a pause. I felt the absence in my bones, the distance from collaborators, from the music, from the cadence of our work in Tanzania.

The work carried on in smaller ways, emails, drafts, digital exchanges, but the living pulse of it was missing.

And then, the world cracked open again.

November 2021. Johannesburg pulsed with beats and defied torrential rains as the ACCES (Africa Conference for Collaborations, Exchange and Showcases) Music Conference roared to life. Lightning split the sky while drums and synths rose from every corner. Visuals were as loud as the audible, hands lifted, bodies swaying under neon light. The crowd was electric, thunder rolling both above and within.

It wasn't just a gathering; it was a testament to endurance. Artists from across continents, all navigating their own storms, bound by one unshakable truth: *music is the universal language.*

For me, it was also something deeply personal. After years apart, I reunited with Alex, the producer who had stood beside me in that small Arusha studio in 2012. Seeing him here, stepping onto his first international stage, was like watching our collaboration take its first breath in a larger world.

I remember the way he stood just inside the conference hall, shoulders square, yet eyes darting as if trying to take in everything at once. The swirl of multilingual conversations, the rhythm of panel discussions, the polished confidence of artists who had traveled the circuit before, all of it pressed in around him.

It reminded me of my own first steps into Tanzania years earlier, wide-eyed, uncertain, but propelled by conviction. Now it was Alex's turn to stand at the threshold of something bigger than either of us could have scripted.

When he turned to me, there was no hesitation, only a quiet smile that said—*We belong here too*.

He dove into the workshops, asked sharp questions during panels, and stayed up late in circles of conversation where strangers became collaborators. Each night, we walked back through rain-slicked streets, replaying the day's sparks: the ideas that startled us, the opportunities that beckoned, the reminders of how far we had come since that dimly lit room above a mechanic's shop.

Just as I had once leapt into his world, he was now leaping into mine, the international stage of cultural exchange. Our journeys, years apart but eerily parallel, converged here under Johannesburg's storm-lit sky.

A Tenth Year, A New Chorus

From that reunion, a new idea took root: a celebratory ten-year anniversary choir album. Not just to mark time, but to leave a legacy.

I reached out to Mokia, our long-time collaborator, to help identify communities that might join in this celebration.

I explained that we hoped to create something inclusive, a choir that reflected both heritage and hope. Without hesitation, he recommended Angel Mollel, a respected community advocate from Hai District whose leadership and warmth had earned deep trust.

When I contacted Angel to ask whether her village might be interested in participating, she didn't hesitate. She immediately embraced the idea and stepped forward as both liaison and coordinator. Through her guidance, singers from Ormelili Village—men and women ranging from fifteen to sixty—gathered to form what would become the Ormelili Choir.

Ormelili Choir gathered, elders with weather-lined faces, youth with fire in their eyes, women balancing grace and strength, men grounding the sound with deep resonance. Their voices filled the studio, harmonies rising like sunlight spilling across a valley after rain, sometimes dazzling, sometimes soft as mist, but always pulsing with something larger than us.

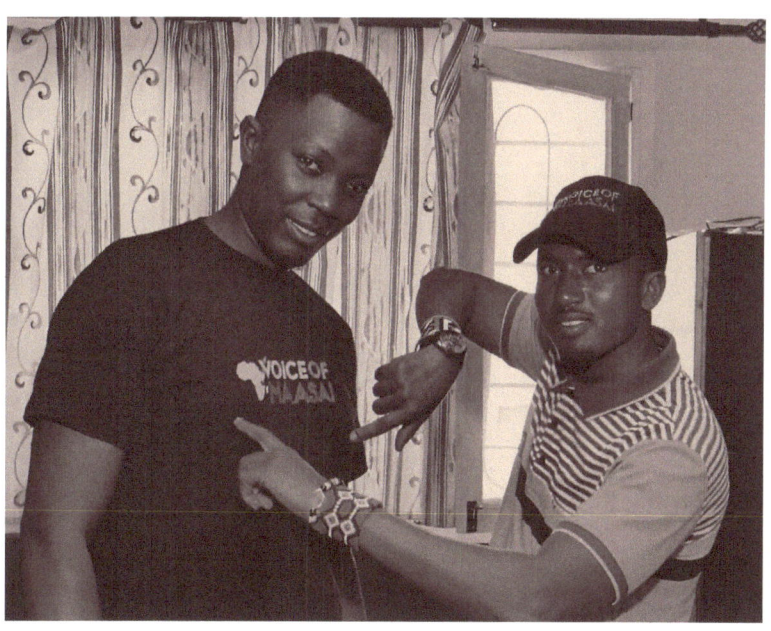

Angel carried herself with quiet authority, the kind that doesn't need to be announced to be felt. Alex was electric as the music took shape, hands flying across the soundboard, ears tuned to every nuance. The songs unfolded with surprising textures; *Upendo* (love) threading itself through Maasai gospel refrains, the sway of Calypso, the rolling hips of Chakacha, the playful bounce of Makirikiri, and the aching bends of Blues.

The tenth year was not a victory lap. It was both a homecoming and a launch.

CHAPTER 11

Dream Team by Design, Not Chance

The first decade taught me something simple yet profound: vision can light a path, but it is people who walk it into reality.

Voice of Maasai became more than a label or a collaboration; it became a living practice of shared responsibility and layered storytelling. My role was not only founder, but listener, provocateur, and quiet gardener of potential. I tried to draw out the brilliance in each teammate, asking questions not for tidy answers, but to uncover new questions they could carry forward themselves.

After nearly three years away during the pandemic, I returned to Tanzania nervous, uncertain whether I would find my rhythm again. I booked accommodation close to the studio, quietly craving a safety net.

Relief and Unspoken Sorrow (March 2023)

Crossing the hotel lobby, I heard my name, faint, almost lost in the clink of cups. I turned, and there he was. Dr. Ole.

He ran toward me, trembling not with weakness but with joy so fierce it pulled him forward. His arms locked around me, tight, unrelenting, pressing the air from my lungs. For five long minutes, neither of us moved. Time folded, years collapsing into the circle of his embrace.

When he finally loosened his grip, his eyes revealed both relief and unspoken sorrow. Over cups of chai gone cold, he shared his story—years imprisoned for rallying behind an opposing political candidate during Magufuli's regime. It wasn't just confinement; it was stolen time, the erosion of freedom, and the shadow of watchfulness that lingered still.

I left that meeting carrying two truths at once: gratitude for his survival, and the sobering awareness that those I cared about here lived daily within a fragile balance, resilience on one side, risk on the other.

Another Light into Another World

Later that week, I honored Alex and his wife, Judy, with a celebratory safari into Ngorongoro Crater. I wanted the landscape itself to say what words could not, the hush as a rhino appeared from the mist, the stride of elephants across the valley floor, the gold light spilling over the rim. My way of saying:

I see you. I see the years you've given, the sacrifices made,

the steady hands guiding this vision forward.

Back in Arusha, we stood before the VOM mural, its colors pulsing, the community's spirit painted on a wall. Momentum seemed to have its own heartbeat. Afterward, I joined their family for dinner.

Laughter filled their small apartment as their nine-year-old son animatedly explained *The Hobbit*. Then, in a quiet shift, he told me his teacher had hit him at

school. His voice was matter-of-fact, but the weight lingered.

Here, joy rarely arrives alone. Celebration walks hand in hand with sorrow, progress with hardship. Life strips away before it builds. And yet, what emerges is not emptiness, but resilience; people living in constant quiet transformation, always prepared for the unpredictable.

To be here is to listen, to learn, to accept that love, progress, and pain often arrive in the same breath, and to choose it all anyway.

A Team Built by Design

As manager, I poured care into shaping not just a roster, but the heartbeat of our resilience; a convergence of talent and tenacity that became the foundation of *Voice of Maasai*.

This dream team, *VOM VIP*, was cultivated, each person bringing a vital thread to the fabric of our label's success:

- **Producer, Writer & Instrumentalist – Alex Lobulu**
  The quiet architect of our sound, shaping each track with precision and authenticity.

- **Lead Male Vocalist & Maasai Community Liaison, Kakesio Village, Ngorongoro District – Nemaa Koshuma**
  His voice carried the cultural pride that gave our work its heartbeat.

- **Lead Female Vocalist & Maasai Community Liaison, Simanjiro, Manyara District – Pendo Moringe**
  Her voice and presence bridged tradition and trust, mentoring others while guiding us through community collaboration.

- **Promotions & Radio Manager – Jeremy Tum**
  He refused to let our songs sit quietly on a shelf—hustling them onto airwaves, into streets, into everyday ears.

- **Culture Liaison & Translator – Dr. Ole Kuney**
  Our steady compass, ensuring meaning was never lost between language and culture.

- **Cultural Guide & Trusted Comrade – Mussa**
  From my earliest days in Moshi, he became my interpreter of Tanzania behind the scenes—reminding me that cultural navigation is its own kind of leadership.

- **Executive Producer & Business Manager – Myself**
  Bringing the entrepreneurial grit to align creativity with systems, ensuring the dream could grow roots.

- **Hype Squad & Support Network – My Family**
  Michael anchoring with steady faith and scrupulous attention to detail, my children pitching in with admin, encouragement, and blunt but needed honesty.

Building the Model

Together, we refined how we worked: open dialogue, shared critique, radical trust. Collaboration was rarely smooth, chaos lurked, perfectionism tempted, but we held a middle ground where creativity could thrive.

Out of that came a model meant to lift everyone:

- Art projects reaching beyond performance into education and awareness.

- Opportunities for artists to travel, teach, and lead.

- Environments built for curiosity and experimentation.

- Systems for shared stewardship and leadership within.

Creative Leadership

My hope was never only that *Voice of Maasai* would change how the world hears Maasai voices. I hoped it would change how young Maasai see themselves: as custodians, innovators, bridge-builders in their own right.

Creative leadership, I've learned, isn't about direction, it's about design. It's about cultivating the conditions where possibility can take root. It asks for deep listening, trust in process, and faith in people.

Within *Voice of Maasai*, that meant collaboration wasn't a courtesy, it was the core. Every project became a dialogue: between tradition and innovation, local insight and global reach, what was dreamed and what could be sustained.

Leadership, in this sense, wasn't about being in front. It was about being among.

Working within Maasai communities meant confronting realities that were complex and often uncomfortable. To move forward responsibly, we had to measure power as carefully as we measured sound; navigate silences, tensions, and unspoken rules that carried equal meaning. Supporting women's voices without dismissing traditional structures required diplomacy and constant recalibration.

We weren't only expanding capacity, we were building with accountability. Every step required balancing vision with vigilance, holding both tradition and transformation. Rewarding fairly. Recognizing contributions honestly. Adapting methods without compromising integrity.

Redefining ROI

Return on investment, for me, has never been measured in profit margins. The true return is found in connection, in voices amplified, opportunities created, and trust earned across distance and difference.

Being a humanitarian, I've learned, isn't about rejecting money. It's about refusing to let money define meaning. Profit may keep the lights on, but purpose is what keeps the fire lit.

Voice of Maasai was built on that principle. Every decision, from royalties to storytelling, has been guided by purpose over profit. The goal was never to chase trends or scale fast, but to build something that could stand on integrity and endure through collaboration. We invested in people before platforms, in process before promotion. Over time, that trust became our greatest asset.

CHAPTER 12

Foundations in Concrete and Community

There is something quietly profound about a circle bound not by contracts, but by purpose. Over the years we became more than collaborators, we became witnesses to each other's grit and grace.

The Spongy Time *(April 2023)*

I start each return to Tanzania with what I call *spongy time*, days meant to absorb. Relearn the cadence of voices, the texture of air, the tug-of-war between memory and the reality in front of me.

It isn't culture shock; I'm no rookie. Years of crossings taught me to anchor in experience even when panic circles the edges. Checklists, short affirmations, and steady daily rituals are not just tools; they're life preservers. (Also: hydration, snacks, and the standing rule that any bad translation goes under "*careful, bicycles*")

Every trip is its own world: new goals, new people, new risks, and a new me, a little older, perspective shifting. Time does not wait. These days always remind me that I'm not returning to a project, I'm returning to a community that keeps reshaping who I am.

From Borrowed Rooms to Brick

For years we worked in borrowed rooms, peeling paint, sagging ceilings, damp seeping in after rain. Street noise bled into takes; power slipped away mid-chorus. We adapted and made beauty anyway. Still, a stubborn dream held: a studio of our own.

The decision was not only bricks and budgets; it was about where to anchor the next chapter. Alex had land, trees shading the yard where his children played. A place close enough for dawn work and family dinners. I knew with clarity: investing here, in him, in them, was how *Voice of Maasai* would deepen. Not charity. Faith. Faith in permanence, stability, and a foundation strong enough to carry voices and livelihoods beyond these walls.

The day we opened the door, fresh paint still hung in the air. Standing in that sunlit room, I felt something I hadn't been able to name in years: relief. Not because the work got easier, it didn't, but because the foundation was no longer mine to hold alone. Alex stood beside me with quiet satisfaction, already hearing the music. Years of patchwork dissolved. This was home, for the work, the mission, and the family who would guard it.

Lyrics, Trust, and A New Voice

For years I had scribbled lyrics on hotel receipts and in the margins of sleepless nights. One day I asked Alex: *What if we bring these to life?* He doesn't just hear words; he listens until the song inside them emerges. His compositions carry the warmth of Tanzanian gospel and instincts rooted deeper than theory. Beginning didn't feel like risk, it felt like coming home.

Then came Pendo. She wasn't scouted; she was entrusted, introduced by a friend who believed in her voice. We met at the Melia: measured introductions at first, her "agent" speaking more than she did. As music entered the conversation, her shoulders dropped. We invited Alex to join on the spot, and by the end of that meeting the path was clear: studio time next.

In the booth, Alex coaxed her into bloom. By day's end it was obvious: she had something worth nurturing. Pendo gave *Voice of Maasai* a fresh tone; feminine, youthful, resonant. A bridge—modern yet rooted, carrying Maasai consciousness into new possibility. Her voice didn't just expand our sound; it expanded my imagination for what *Voice of Maasai* could become when women stepped to the center of it.

The momentum of 2023 set 2024 in motion under one word: Dream. It became our guide as we opened the studio to new voices.

Dream As Compass, Community Talent Show *(Feb 2024)*

Our most ambitious project yet: the first talent search in Simanjiro District, not in polished halls, but in the dust and pulse of community life. Months of prep tested us. Permits stalled. Heat pressed down; insects pressed in. The generator flirted with melodrama. A motorbike broke on the road to Lobosiret. Each snag was another knot to loosen, and the team kept improvising with sweat and stubborn resolve. (Somewhere in there, flowers arrived from my husband: *To my beautiful executive producer bride*. Life balance, global edition.)

From my makeshift "apartment HQ" in Arusha, I juggled schedules and calls until the team reached the village. Then none of that mattered. The welcome was warm and unguarded. By mid-morning, eighty-nine participants stood ready, some walking miles, others arriving by motorbike. Dust hovered, goats bleated, anticipation crackled.

Contestants faced three challenges:

- a freestyle song without accompaniment—raw and unadorned

- a hymn or familiar piece—to test blend and discipline

- an improvised performance to pre-arranged music—where creativity met courage

We listened for range, pitch, timing, and harmony, and for something harder to name: presence, the ability to hold a space and make it matter.

By day's end, ten finalists emerged across three villages, each receiving a small stipend for food and transport and an invite to the Winners' Round in Lobosiret. On the final morning, nerves trembled until the team rallied contestants, jumping, laughing, shaking out fear. Then came the music: tentative, confident, soaring, trembling, voices climbing into the Tanzanian sky.

When the three winners were called, their smiles seemed wide enough to catch the sun:

- **Jonas Eliya** (Lobosiret)
- **Nai Yohana** (Narakawo
- **Lamayani Tangwai** (Lobosiret)

Training began at once. Alex guided with patience and precision. Pendo mentored with warmth, helping them navigate cultural nuance and discover confidence in the studio. What had begun as raw potential was now stepping into permanence: our new studio, alive with its first generation of voices.

Celebrations and Sorrows

After the talent competition, we gathered at Alex and Judy's for a meal, laughter spilling into the evening as their eldest surprised us with a visit and the youngest giggled from the next room.

Then joy made room for grief. News of Alex's nephew, just twenty, lost suddenly to cerebral malaria. Soon after came word of Nemaa's daughter's injury. Power cuts and broken internet made the distances feel longer, the losses heavier. Loss tests the seams of any vision, but that week I learned our work wasn't fragile; our people were strong enough to carry one another.

Here, joy and sorrow travel together, close as shadow and light. I once tried to untangle that knot. Now I see it as the gift: binding joy to grief, risk to resilience, people to one another.

Woven Across Oceans

I've learned that a small circle, when bound by purpose, can move mountains. We stumbled, improvised, and lifted one another through moments that could have easily unraveled us. Each person added a thread—some bright, some quiet—but together, the weave held. I used to think leadership meant carrying the heaviest part; now I know it's letting others strengthen the places you can't.

And the threads stretched far beyond Tanzania. Across oceans, friends believed without fanfare. They offered design help, donations, critiques, encouragement; whatever they had to give. Family lent time and humor, steadying me through late nights and thin margins. No one asked for credit; belief was its own reward.

The studio walls became more than brick and paint; they were fairness made tangible. Proof that imagination can stand upright when built on shared ground, that you don't need perfect conditions, just people willing to show up and work together.

That's what this has always been: creativity as currency.

Share the Win: From Foundations to Portfolio

Looking back, it's hard to trace exactly where momentum became movement. Somewhere between dusty roads, broken cables, and too many cups of green tea, a fragile idea grew its own spine. What began as a single encounter under an acacia tree had evolved into something living; sustained by belief, built by many hands.

We didn't arrive here by grand design. We built it piece by piece, everyone contributing something of value, everyone walking away a little richer in spirit.

By the time our own walls stood firm, the story had shifted. This was no longer a dream I was shepherding, it was a movement we were building together. Music carried more than melody; it carried trust, risk, and the quiet courage of people choosing to believe in one another.

Part V turns toward the field notes and lessons learned, but this chapter marks a different kind of threshold. The foundations aren't just concrete; they're relational. They were poured by many hands, across many miles, held together by fairness and imagination; values that shaped me long before Tanzania, back on Fair Street.

And even now, standing inside this hard-earned milestone, I feel it: the next movement forming. Creation, after all, is never finished. It only asks us to keep stepping toward the people brave enough to build with us.

> "
> *Every song begins as breath, a vibration in the chest before it finds shape in sound.*

PART 5

Lessons Learned: Field Notes & Practical Takeaways

Business Credo: How We Went from Idea to Music Label —— 102
Closing Notes ———————————————————— 109

Business Credo: How We Went from Idea to Music Label

Years of cross-cultural work, creative collaboration, and trial by fire have shaped how I operate today. Every partnership, setback, and success taught me something about structure, the kind that protects creativity rather than constrains it. None of these principles were drafted in a boardroom; they were forged in real time, through long nights, tangled logistics, shared risk, and the slow work of earning trust.

Develop a Credo

Our C-Factor Credo
A guiding principle that strengthens our productive, collaborative, and creativity-driven community.

Creativity builds confidence. Confidence shapes character. Character strengthens community.

Tenets To Follow

- **Listen more, talk less.** How well you listen determines how far you go.
- **Lead with creativity, inclusion, and teamwork.** Design spaces where people feel seen, heard, and empowered to contribute.

- **Align tasks with talent.** Match skills to responsibilities.

- **Build clear processes** that foster accountability and trust.

- **Cultivate stewardship.** Everyone is responsible for shared resources and results.

- **Manage the management.** Leadership must model the same integrity it expects.

- **Illuminate mistakes**, don't cement them. Learn, adjust, and move forward.

- **Balance quality with cultural flexibility.** Hold standards high, but stay responsive to context.

Delegate Responsibilities

Create the Dream Team: *Value in Diversity*
Strong teams are built by recognizing and integrating different kinds of intelligence and strength.

Skill Set 1: *Reactive/Sensory/Non-Verbal*
Ability to read environments and relationships quickly; build rapport through observation and presence.

Skill Set 2: *Proactive/Conceptual/Verbal*
Ability to negotiate, articulate ideas clearly, and communicate productively across differences.

Skill Set 3: *Connector/Influencer/Strategist*
Ability to leverage networks, create synergy, and scale collaborative work with purpose.

Define Expectations

Zero Tolerance Policy
No verbal, physical, or written abuse toward any *Voice of Maasai* representative, contractor, or collaborator will be tolerated. Respect is non-negotiable.

Handling Difficult Clients/Partners
Set the tone early. Model professionalism. Define what respectful collaboration looks like—for both sides.

Cross-Cultural Collaboration: How to Not Finetune a Fiasco

- **Start with Listening, Not Leading** Enter new spaces without assuming authority. Absorb the cadence of voices, silences, and gestures before taking action.

  Story: When I first arrived in Tanzania, I had no roadmap, no title. My only tools were humility and presence. I learned to sit through silences, letting others set the rhythm, before I dared to speak.

- **Respect Hierarchies, But Notice Silences**
  Learn how power shapes who speaks and who decides. Pay as much attention to who is not heard as to who is.

  Story: In rehearsals, men stood up front while women carried the sound. I had to understand the patriarchal structure while quietly creating space that recognized and uplifted women's leadership within it.

- **Adapt Communication Styles** Adjust tone, timing, and approach to match cultural context. What feels like efficiency in one culture may read as disrespect in another.

Story: I once jumped into scheduling without proper greetings, and the room fell silent. Skipping relational warm-up felt dismissive. When I adjusted—starting with check-ins and small courtesies—meetings immediately became smoother and more cooperative.

- **Anchor in Relationships, Not Transactions**
  Progress isn't built on contracts alone, it's built on trust forged through repeated presence, shared meals, and showing up when it matters.

  Story: A bread vendor on a bicycle ended up saving our rehearsal. When I realized the choir hadn't eaten, we bought ten loaves and sweet tea on the spot. That small, shared meal did more than solve hunger—it signaled presence, care, and commitment. Moments like that built more trust than any contract ever could.

- **Reward Genuine Goodwill**
  Recognize and support those who align with the mission, while stepping away quietly from those pursuing self-interest.

  Story: When a collaborator tried to claim ownership and walked off with CDs, I let it go. Escalation cost more than it solved. Protecting the mission meant investing in those who showed integrity, not fighting self-interest.

- **Value Improvisation as Much as Planning**
  Expect taxis not to arrive, power to cut, or food to run out. Flexibility isn't failure, it's part of the rhythm of collaboration.
  Story: Power cuts, goats, and storms paused sessions regularly. Adapting with diplomatic steadiness helped me see improvisation as genuine collaboration, not a failure of preparation.

- **Protect Integrity Over Perfection**
  A few lost CDs or small setbacks aren't disasters if the larger mission stays intact. Integrity builds longevity.

Story: I once felt pressure to refine the songs for Western listeners. Choosing to keep them unadorned honored their dignity. Integrity—not perfection—became the measure that protected the mission.

- **Hold Accountability with Grace**
  Set clear expectations around quality, finances, and roles, but deliver correction with diplomacy to preserve relationships.

  Story: Missteps were inevitable. When receipts didn't match expenses, I corrected it firmly but without shame—resetting clear financial boundaries while preserving the relationships that made the collaboration strong.

- **Build Systems that Empower, Not Override**
  Create frameworks for collaboration that amplify local voices and ownership, rather than imposing external control.

  Story: Kickstarter wasn't just about raising funds, it was about proving viability and setting up a framework for collaboration. Every dollar pledged built not just an album, but a system where voices could travel farther.

- **Stay Conscious of Privilege** Acknowledge the freedoms you bring as an outsider may not be available to collaborators. Lead with humility and awareness.
  Story: I never forgot my freedom to cross borders wasn't theirs. Their risks were different. That awareness meant I couldn't impose my vision—I had to co-create our shared reality.

- **Recognize the Knot of Joy and Grief**
  In Tanzania, celebration and sorrow often arrive together. Learn to live inside that knot, rather than trying to untangle it.

  Story: In one week we celebrated the birth of new music and mourned the loss of a family member to malaria. I learned that in Tanzania, joy and sorrow walk side by side. The knot isn't meant to be untangled, it's meant to be lived.

Compass: Self-Imposed Rules for Staying the Course

In cross-cultural work, success isn't about scale, it's about staying aligned. These are the compass points that have kept me steady through collaboration, chaos, and cultural negotiation.

- **Notice Patterns, Name Power, Refuse the Hero Costume**
  Pay attention to who holds influence, who carries invisible weight, and how credit circulates. Build with, not about.

- **Safety, Recognition, Belonging**
  I believe the heart of both humanity and creativity rests on these three pillars:

  1. Safety, because collaboration shrivels when people feel exposed.

  2. Recognition (yes, vanity too) because everyone deserves to be seen.

  3. Belonging, because without it, even the strongest voice goes unheard.

- **Define What Humanitarian Means to You**
  Being a humanitarian isn't about rejecting money; it's about refusing to let money define meaning. Profit might keep the lights on, but purpose is what keeps the fire lit.

- **A Model for Creative Endeavor**
  Over time, we built a framework where creativity and care could coexist:

  1. Art projects that reach beyond performance into education and awareness.

  2. Opportunities for artists to travel, teach, and lead.

  3. Environments designed for curiosity and experimentation.

  4. Systems of shared stewardship and leadership within.

True collaboration lives at the intersection of purpose and permission, where everyone feels safe to risk, recognized for trying, and rooted enough to stay.

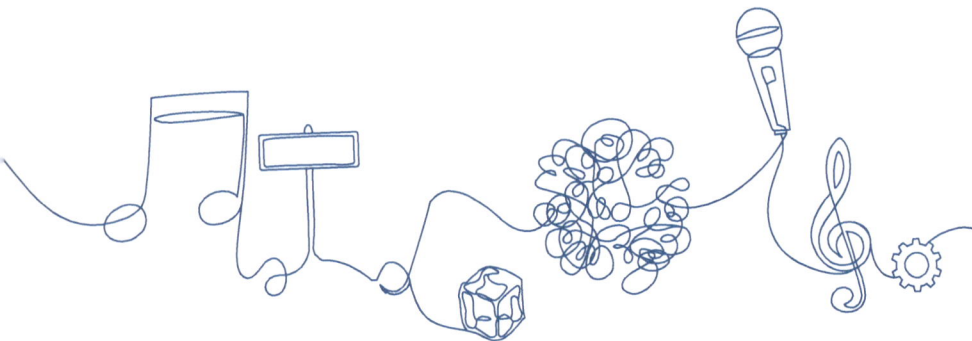

Closing Notes

What began on Fair Street—a knack for bartering, building, and believing in people—grew into something larger than music. It became a circle of voices pulling up chairs, sharing breath, and carrying culture forward with grit, grace, and laughter.
Our success was never measured in charts or streams; it was defined by the bridges we forged, and the trust strengthened along the way. What remains is the bond; imperfect, enduring, alive.

This was never about wealth or acclaim; it was about offering what sustains and creating what connects. The memoir doesn't mark the start of the work, it simply names what has already been built and clears the path for what comes next.

If Volume I is the story of how *Voice of Maasai* was built, then Volume II is the story of what lives inside it, the voices, the albums, the artists, the art. If this book has been the backbone, the next is the heartbeat.

The movement continues, and we turn the page together.

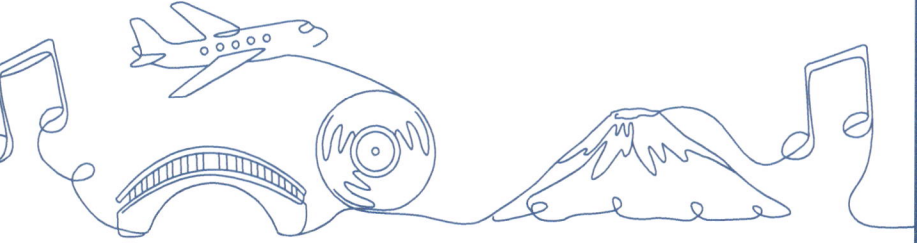

Acknowledgments

Writing this book has been a staggering amount of work, and also a gift. It allowed me to relive a transformative journey with fresh perspective and renewed gratitude. None of it would have been possible without the people who walked beside me, offering their energy, expertise, and faith when I needed it most.

To my steadfast team, **Alex Lobulu**, **Jeremy Tum**, **Nemaa Koshuma**, **Pendo Moringe**, you are more than collaborators; you are my family. Together, we've recorded in studios where power cut out mid-take, crossed rough roads with songs still echoing in our heads, and dreamed up possibilities bigger than the circumstances around us. Your resilience, creativity, and unshakable belief have lit the path forward again and again, even when the way seemed uncertain.

To **Dr. Ole Kuney**, thank you for walking beside me through cultural nuance with patience and wisdom. You translated more than words; you interpreted worlds. Your friendship has been a compass, helping me navigate unfamiliar landscapes of protocol, tradition, and trust. With you, doors opened, misunderstandings softened, and I learned how to step more carefully, more respectfully, in spaces not my own.

To **Mussa Kijuu**, thank you for driving me across Tanzania on roads that stretched through dust, rain, and endless horizons. You kept me safe in moments that could have unraveled, and with every stop you opened doors into villages, families, and countless local lives I would never have reached alone. Through your generosity, I came to know your homeland not as a visitor, but as a student. You helped me find my footing in landscapes and communities that were new to me, grounding adventure with trust and friendship.

To the **Pristine Trails team**, thank you for your years of committed hospitality, guiding us through savannahs alive with lion calls, across riverbeds marked by elephant prints, and into sunsets that seemed to set the whole sky aflame. From our earliest safaris to the unforgettable celebration of our ten-year anniversary, your care and expertise made every journey feel both daring and safe, wild and welcoming. You are the best.

To **Arusha Meru International School**, thank you for opening your walls to our vision and allowing the mural to become part of your everyday landscape. Your generosity created space for art to live where young minds gather and grow.

To **Rukia Kurwa**, thank you for being the architect of possibility. Your persistence, skill, and grace in negotiating made this project not only possible but meaningful, ensuring the mural stands as a bridge between creativity and community.

To **Jacqueline (Jax) Mennenoh**, thank you for your design excellence and the many years of shared creative vision. From the early days of *Voice of Maasai* to the polished pages now in hand, you've been a constant creative ally. From late-night brainstorms to the careful formatting and thoughtful design choices that give this book its shape, your fingerprints are everywhere. What could have been a solitary process became collaborative joy because of your insight, patience, and generosity. I'm grateful not only for the beauty you helped bring to life here, but for the sisterhood and trust woven into every step.

To all our **Kickstarter supporters**, thank you for daring to believe in a dream before it had proof. Your pledges were more than contributions; they were acts of faith that turned an improbable idea into a living movement. Every song, every story, every note carried forward is indebted to your early trust and generosity.

To **Christine Style**, thank you for seeing my potential early on and championing me for the artist's grant that set so much of this in motion.

To **Dara Larson**, thank you for being a mentor to my younger artist-self, planting seeds of courage that continue to grow.

To **Diane Schroeder**, I'm grateful for your friendship, critical eye, and encouragement at every stage.

To **Myles (Mush) Berman**, thank you for your steadfast support and relentless networking, you opened doors I could never have reached alone.

I also want to thank those I met during my **NOLS (National Outdoor Leadership School) expedition**, especially **Lynn Petzold**, for your steady leadership and for stretching the way I think, and **Jasmine Shaw**, for hosting the memorable radio program in Sitka, Alaska, where you featured *Voice of Maasai* and its impact on Native culture.

To my husband, **Michael Cicchella**—thank you for being both my steadfast cheerleader and my clearest compass. Your confidence in my solo travels gave me the courage to keep saying yes to bold, arduous journeys, and your steady counsel reminded me that vision is strongest when grounded in partnership.

And to my children, **Kyle Vigue**, **Niosha Vigue**, **Angelina Cicchella**, **Carmen Cicchella**, thank you for your insights, shameless promotions, and for rolling up your sleeves alongside me. From proofing copy to brainstorming album art to working events, you've been part of everything. This work carries your fingerprints too, and I hope you feel it.

To my sisters, **Jacqueline Mennenoh** and **Jennifer Versch**, thank you for the laughter, memories, and probing questions that have shaped both the work and the life behind it.

To **Ardis** and **Mike Cicchella Sr.**, thank you for believing in this work from the very start. Your support, curiosity, and generosity have carried me more than you know, reminding me that bold ideas take root best when family tends the soil.

About the
Author & Founder

Jessey Jansen is a Creative Leader and Social Entrepreneur whose work is shaped by early life on Fair Street, where resourcefulness and imagination first took root. She built her professional foundation in marketing, branding, communication, and visual art; fields that sharpened her instinct for narrative, diplomacy, strategic thinking for low-resource ventures, and the power of a well-made story.

Those skills carried her to Tanzania, where she founded *Voice of Maasai* and forged a long-standing cross-cultural creative partnership. Blending design thinking with ethical storytelling, her practice centers on collaboration, cultural respect, citizen diplomacy and art made in community for long-lasting impact.

Jessey lives between Seattle and Austin, traveling regularly to Tanzania to continue recording, mentoring, and tending the creative bridges sparked in her small hometown.

About the Book Designer

Jacqueline (Jax) Mennenoh is an accomplished Photographer, Creative Director and Graphic Designer with over 25 years of experience shaping award-winning visual identities across print, digital, and experiential platforms. Known for her ability to combine strategic thinking with refined aesthetics, she has led creative direction for diverse brands, campaigns, and projects—translating complex ideas into compelling visual narratives.

Her design work has been recognized for its balance, clarity, and storytelling power, reflecting a deep understanding of composition and communication. With a career rooted in both artistry and strategy, Jax brings a holistic approach to design—ensuring every project is not only visually striking, but also purposeful and enduring.

Use what you have, make it count, and share the win. It's how small beginnings become movements.

www.ingramcontent.com/pod-product-compliance
Ingram Content Group UK Ltd.
Pitfield, Milton Keynes, MK11 3LW, UK
UKHW060125240426
12049UKWH00012B/156